MarkTruth™

The Truth About Self-Publishing Your Book

I0170272

By Mark T. Arsenault

The Truth About Self-Publishing Your Book

Gold Rush Publishing

PO Box 582155

Elk Grove, CA 95758

916-572-4478

E-mail: goldrushpub@gmail.com

www.GoldRushPub.com

The Truth About Self-Publishing Your Book and MarkTruth are trademarks owned by Mark T. Arsenault.

Visit **MarkTruth.com** for free inspirational, motivational and instructional material.

Cover design by Mark T. Arsenault

Cover illustration (source)

Library of Congress Control Number: 2016915614

ISBN: 978-1-890305-12-3 paperback

Printed in USA

Contents

"A mind needs books as a sword needs a whetstone if it is to keep its edge."

—*George R. R. Martin*

Part One:

Who Should Read This Book?

Obviously, this book is for anyone who wants to self-publish their book. That one's obvious. But what sort of person should consider self-publishing their own book?

Anyone who has exhausted all other publishing options. There are a lot of options for publishing a book. Many of them are time-consuming and result in lots more rejection than acceptance.

Anyone who wants to retain full rights to their work. Signing a publishing deal with a traditional publisher means signing over some of your rights.

Anyone who wants to earn more money than with traditional publishing. In a nutshell, compare a 10% royalty from a traditional publisher versus 50% of retail (if selling at wholesale prices to a distributor) or a 70% royalty paid for eBook sales.

Anyone who wants to get paid faster. It can take three to six months to receive royalties on books sold in the traditional "book trade," compared to as little as one month with epublishing.

Anyone who wants to publish their book quickly. Once your book is laid out and ready to print, it can take as little as a few weeks from when you upload the files for the book to be available for sale online and available to booksellers.

Anyone who wants complete control of their book. In the traditional or "legacy" publishing, rewrites can be required by the agent or publisher, cover design and marketing is controlled by the publisher, etc. When you self-publish, it's all in your hands.

Anyone who writes a book in an obscure genre. If your book is perceived as only reaching a very small market, a traditional publisher will likely pass on it. By self-publishing, you ensure its existence!

Anyone who's "looking for their audience." As with niche products, it may be that you haven't yet found raving fans for your book. By self-publishing, you ensure your book is available for when you've found them (and when new fans find your book).

Anyone who wants to "be on the right side of history." Digital book sales are on par with paper book sales. In some cases, they surpass paper book sales. The use of smartphones to access the internet and to read eBooks is growing. It's best to be a part of the new age than to lag behind.

Anyone who already has an audience. If you have a bunch of fans of your blog or you have a following from your public performances or some such, you can take advantage of your built-in audience to promote your books.

Anyone who wants to publish a collection or anthology. Perhaps you have a collection of short stories or poems on your website. Although popular in general, anthologies and collections without well-known contributors may not be popular with publishers.

Anyone who wants to republish out of print books. Authors with a number of older, out-of-print books can resurrect them and find a new audience for them.

Anyone who wants to prioritize time management. Spending time pursuing a literary agent and/or publisher can be very time-consuming. Some authors may prefer to get their book into print, even though it means supporting it themselves.

Authors of personal or family projects. This is another niche product, with limited market appeal. Perhaps the project is solely meant to be given to family members as gifts. In either case, it's an excellent candidate for self-publishing.

Anyone who wants the challenge of learning how. There's a learning curve to complete some of the tasks related to self-publishing but some folks are not only up to the challenge, they enjoy it!

Authors who are "building their platform." Self-publishing gives subject matter experts credibility and allows them to build their brand, increase their followers on social media, and so on.

Anyone who wants to gain credibility. Some folks want to boost their credibility and position themselves as an authority in their field. Writing and publishing a book can help do that.

"Books are the treasured wealth of the world and the fit inheritance of generations and nations."

—*Henry David Thoreau*

Part Two:

Top 10 Reasons to Self-Publish Your Book

I first began my journey into self-publishing back in 1996. I had worked on a few projects as a freelance author and became friends with several publishers. I was very interested in the process and started learning about it from my friends in the industry. The more I learned the more I realized the value of being a publisher instead of simply an author. There's nothing wrong with being an author. Don't get me wrong. But the reality was – and still *is* – that there are advantages to being a publisher. Here are ten of the biggest reasons to self-publish your book, in my humble opinion (and in no particular order).

1. Maintain Complete Control of Your Book

Let's face it. We creative types love our work. When we create something it's like giving birth to it. Our books become almost like living entities in our mind. That's why artists, car enthusiasts, and others refer to something they love as their "baby." Our books are no different.

The problem is, all that emotional investment in our work isn't shared by agents and publishers. Our "babies" are just things in the business of publishing. It may be a good manuscript or even a *great* manuscript, but it's still a "thing" in the business world. Unless an author is a well-established name in the industry, he or she will have almost no input, let alone control, over their work once in the publisher's hands. Authors traditionally don't get to pick the book's cover, set the retail price, or have input on the interior design and fonts used in the book (also known as layout). You won't have any say over the dust-jacket copy, ads, marketing pitch, or overall budget. You'll have zero influence over where your book is distributed, or for how long. And subtle terms in your book contract can be ticking bombs. Without warning, your publisher may even drop your book—or you, as one of their house authors.

Some writers don't like the idea of edits. They just don't want editors going through their work and changing it. They don't want to spend time in rewrites, and they especially do not want people telling them how or what to write.

2. Retain the Rights to Your Work

In the traditional publishing world, contracts can be complicated. The sheer complexity of negotiating a publishing contract can be overwhelming for anyone, especially those with no experience with such things. To put it mildly, publishing contracts can be confusing and intimidating. Without a background in law (particularly contract law) it's easy to sign away secondary and subsidiary rights indefinitely. Those rights could mean a lot of lost revenue if a book is very successful. By self-publishing, you retain all of the rights to your work.

3. Get Your Book Published Quickly

With traditional publishing, it can take a comparatively long time to get a manuscript published. The saying "time is money" is true for authors, too. Many publishers require authors to submit their manuscript through an agent. It can take months of query letters just to locate an agent willing to take you on. Agents willing to take on unknowns are out there, but the reality is that it's easier to market a "known commodity." That is an author who already has a recognizable name or face (think some form of celebrity). This is understandable and not insurmountable, just another factor to consider.

Once you find an agent willing to take you on, you then must negotiate a contract. Once the contracts are done and signed, you must develop an acceptable "pitch" that your agent will send to publishers. The agent may ask you to revise your book before submitting it to publishers (because the agent knows what publishers are looking for).

Submitting your manuscript to publishers is the next step in the process. As I've mentioned, many authors face many rejections before ever getting a manuscript picked up by a publisher. In the event, your agent locates an interested publisher, contract negotiations may take quite weeks or maybe months. The publisher may then insist on minor edits or major rewrites of your book. Once the book is approved it goes into their publishing schedule. Long lead times, especially with big publishers, can mean a year, year and a half, or even longer before your book rolls off the presses.

So, if you're very lucky, you might be looking at as much as two years from the time you query agents until you see your book sitting on store shelves (if they buy it, of course).

By self-publishing, you can skip this process and publish your manuscript in book form much more quickly. It's possible to submit your book files and have your book "live" and available to buy online and available to booksellers in less than one month.

4. Earn More Money

In traditional publishing, authors earn royalties (a percentage of each book sale). The percentage is relatively low compared to self-publishing, especially for "eBooks" (electronic books).

In the past, a 10% royalty was typically reserved for the "big time authors," with an advance on royalties of expected sales. Some authors might earn less. Why? Publishers have additional costs involved in bringing books to market. This includes paying for printing and marketing. Essentially, the publishers are taking all of the financial risks. And most books don't do gangbuster sales. So, even at 10% of retail price, a fiction novel selling for $7.99 would result in 80 cents in royalties for the author for each copy sold. For authors whose books sell 100,000 copies, that's a good income! Unfortunately, most authors can't expect that kind of sales numbers, especially without a big publishing house to market the book!

Today, many self-published authors publish their books through "the big online bookseller," both in print and online in electronic format. As of the time this book was written, authors are paid as much as 70% of the retail price of their eBooks for each sale. That's many times more than traditional publishers pay and there's little financial risk for the author. Let's consider that 20 of that seller's overall Top 100 Best Selling ebooks were indie titles priced between $2.99 and $5.99. (*Source: Authorearnings.com, February 2016*). Let's say you price your eBook book at $5.99. You would receive $4.14 for each sale. If you were to sell even 1,000 copies of that book each month you would be earning an extra $4,140 a month!

5. Get Paid Faster

In the traditional book publishing industry, it was common for bookstores to buy books, receive them, and not have to pay the distributor for those books until 90 days had gone by. And any unsold books could be returned to the distributor for a full refund (a practice that, according to *New Yorker* magazine, one exbookseller employee called "an absurdly inefficient model, worse than my uncle sending his laundry home from college.") All of this had to happen before the distributors could report final numbers to the publishers. You can see why authors sometimes weren't paid for months after the sale of a book! This is why royalty "advances" were sometimes paid to an author, especially if the book was believed to be a potential big seller!

When you self-publish, there is still some delay regarding sales of paper books but you have the option of not allowing returns. This can result in fewer books sold, of course. Electronic book sales can be tracked in virtual real time, however. Distributors of eBooks, such as *Kindle Direct Publishing* and print-on-demand (POD) services such as Ingram's *Lightning Source* and *CreateSpace*, report your sales almost immediately and they pay your royalties monthly, with less "lag" from the time of the sales.

6. Take Advantage of Trends

On January 10, 2016, 4 of the Top 10 Best Selling ebooks on a major online bookseller were self-published indie titles! 10 of its overall Top 20 Best Sellers were self-published titles. This trend reached into the Top 100, as 56 of its Best Selling eBooks were self-published indie titles. That's a little more than half! (*Source: Authorearnings.com, February 2016*)

Paper book sales are no longer in decline, as of 2016, they're growing, but the fact remains that ebooks are a large part of the book-buying market. Even if you, as an author, would prefer to see your book in printed format, you'd be well advised to consider releasing an electronic format as well. As I told one coaching client, "If your paper book sells 10,000 copies but another 5,000 people would buy a copy if it were available on *Kindle* and other devices, why ignore those additional sales?"

7. Republish a Backlist

Some successful authors have made additional sales among their growing audiences by reviving and self-publishing their older titles long after they've gone out of print. This assumes the publishing rights to said books either reverted to them or they never relinquished those rights. Their fans may already know the book and no doubt some of them are looking to buy it. If you have older books that have gone out of print, such books are excellent candidates for self-publishing.

8. Other Publishing Options Are Impractical

Authors who have been pounding the proverbial pavement and submitting their manuscript to publishers and/or agents and just haven't been getting any bites. Granted, rejection is part of the game. Countless hugely successful authors will tell you that their first work was rejected dozens if not hundreds of times before being picked up. There's value in persistence. If you want to see your book in print, however, and you don't want to stay in the "rejection mill" game, then self-publishing may be for you.

The flip side to the earlier statement is that there are many stories of writers who finally got fed up with the traditional publishing industry and did it themselves. The upside is that with today's technology, it's never been easier to self-publish. Anyone can do it! (The downside, of course, is that it's never been easier to self-publish. Anyone can do it.)

9. Publishing a Book in a Niche Genre

Authors of works in an extremely unique genre or of particularly obscure topics that relatively few people are interested may choose to self-publish. If an author is writing a book about restoring 19th-century Greek fishing boats, they might consider self-publishing as an option for getting their book in print.

One of the great things about the internet, however, is that it makes finding your audience easier than ever. Thanks to search engines like Google, Yahoo, Bing and YouTube (You didn't know YouTube was a search tool? There's another nugget for you. More on that later.) And the use of hashtags and keywords, it's easier than ever to locate other people who are interested in the things we're passionate about.

Similarly, publishing a collection of poetry or stories or an anthology could be a great project to self-publish. Perhaps you run a blog dedicated to books or a literary website that publishes stories and poetry. Like the expert above, you may have a following but most traditional publishers don't usually look at these kinds of books. It's a niche market, to be sure. That's not to say that collections of stories or anthologies won't sell. They certainly can, especially if you have a popular author or two among the contributors! By self-publishing these titles, you can receive maximum benefit for getting the work into print.

People who create a family genealogy project and wish to publish it in book form are excellent candidates for self-publishing. Likewise, authors who write a lengthy history of their family, a book of anecdotes or stories about their family, primarily for their family members, will often self-publish. You may not expect a great number of sales from such a project. Perhaps you're only intending to print a limited number of copies to give away as gifts. These are all great reasons to self-publish.

10. Building Your Brand

Authors who are building their platform – creating and growing a "brand" and name recognition for themselves – are excellent candidates for self-publishing. For authors who aren't well-known yet, becoming a published author can help establish their credibility and establish them as an expert in their field.

Regardless how easy it is to self-publish these days, the reality is that most people see published authors as having some credibility. It's an accomplishment that many people, themselves, say they aspire to. It can be seen as part of the puzzle when it comes to building a brand.

Want a few more reasons? I threw in a few more for good measure. (It's always better to under promise and over-deliver!)

11. Do It for the Challenge

To some people, learning how to do something is extremely satisfying. That was me back in the mid-'90s. I knew that publishing books would require learning a number of new skills and require time and patience. But I was up for the task and craved the knowledge. I simply wanted to learn how to do it, despite having other publishers tell me it wasn't worth it (true story!). Today I believe, more than ever, that self-publishing is worth the time and effort to learn. This is partially because it's now easier than it's ever been.

12. Find Your Audience

In traditional publishing, the production, marketing, distribution, and sales infrastructure are expensive to maintain. Thus, the process demands new titles be released and placed on bookstore shelves (and other public retail outlets). Because of the expense of maintaining that infrastructure, retail shelf space is very valuable, indeed. Each book title has to have enough sales to justify taking up that space, otherwise, it's quickly replaced by a book that will. (Have you ever wondered why even best-sellers sometimes disappear so soon after they're released? Now, you know.) The average book may sit on the shelf for six-to-eight weeks before a new title replaces it. Most books don't last that long.

Self-published books never have to go "out of print" (OOP). In fact, they only go out of print if the publisher chooses to make it unavailable. Self-published authors have much more time to "find their readers," so to speak. Even so-called "backlist" titles (books that are long out of print or books that didn't sell well at launch) can suddenly see new sales and become bestsellers, thanks to the benefits e-publishing!

13. Reach an Existing Audience

Authors who already have a large audience to whom they can promote their book can confidently self-publish a book – perhaps even a bestselling book – themselves. Let's take, for example, someone who's a well-known host of an infomercial, an industry "expert" or the host of a popular blog. Their experience or their field of authority may not be attractive to mainstream, traditional book publishers. Still, they might have hundreds of thousands of followers. Not all of them are likely to be raving fans, but surely there's a percentage who would buy a product if asked. Self-publishing and promoting your book to these followers just makes sense.

"Sit down to write what you have thought, and not to think about what you shall write."

—*William Cobbett*

Part Three:

What Should I Write About?

It may be that you've already written your book. If that's the case, congratulations are in order! Most people who talk about writing a book never do. The fact that you actually wrote it puts you head and shoulders above the crowd.

Perhaps you're reading this and you don't have a finished manuscript yet, but you know what you're going to write about. Writing a book is itself a process. It takes a fair amount of discipline and work, banging away at the keyboard until you're finished. My advice is to set aside time every day to write.

If either of these describes your situation, you *could* skip ahead to the next appropriate chapter and continue reading. I'm going to recommend you continue reading this and the following chapters, regardless.

Why Continue Reading?

The fact is you're very likely to learn some important information about the publishing process that will help you when it comes to planning your *next* book. You *are* planning to write another book, right? Of course, you are!

If you're like most of the readers of this book, however, it's likely that you haven't yet written your book. Chances are you already have an idea in mind. Fiction or non-fiction, memoir or science fiction novel; the subject can be as varied as there are ideas.

"You're right," you may be thinking. "I haven't written my book yet. In fact, I don't even know what to write about!"

That's okay. I'm here to help.

Picking a Subject to Write About

My first suggestion to anyone who wants to write a book is to write about what they're passionate about. Why?

My experience tells me when someone is passionate about something, they spend more time learning about it and mastering skills associated with that thing.

For example, if someone is passionate about soccer (known as football outside of the United States), they're more likely to read and learn the rules of the game, follow one or more teams or players, and to attend professional soccer events. Someone who's passionate about the sport is going to have an energy and enthusiasm that someone without a passion simply won't have. And this passion comes through in their writing. I can't explain it. It's simply the truth.

Having passion about a subject will move you to do research on the subject so you can include relevant facts and timely information in your book. If you need to spend 20 hours researching something, someone with passion will knock out the research in as short a time as possible, whereas someone lacking that passion is apt to quit because the project is "too hard." While passion itself doesn't equal quality, passion is more likely to lead to quality work than a lack of passion.

I'm Passionate about Many Things. Now What?

Maybe you're more mercenary in your approach to writing a book, meaning you'll write and publish a book about anything that will sell well. How do you determine what's likely to be a good seller? Visit an online bookseller (you know which one) and start perusing the various subjects, with an eye toward how many titles are in each one. Then look at the sale numbers for the top 10 or 20 titles in that category. You'll get an idea of where demand is higher and the herd of titles is not as thick as in other subjects.

I'm Not a Great Writer, But I Can Talk!

My suggestion is to buy a digital recorder that you can slip into your pocket until you need it. Something like the Olympus WS-852, which has a direct USB connector, works great. Then, when the inspiration hits you, pull it out and start dictating your book. Just tell your story. Don't worry about the order of the chapters, or forgetting details at this stage. Just get it all out of your head and onto an .mp3 file.

Then, hire a freelance transcriber to turn all of that talking into a text file or Word document. Then you have something to edit, update, and reorder to your heart's content!

"But, Mark," you're thinking, "where can I find a freelance transcriber? And how am I supposed to afford that?"

Freelancers can be found who do work cheap. Sites like fiverr.com are full of people, especially those in other countries, who will do work like that for as little as five dollars per "gig." You'll need to buy multiple gigs but it's still worth the price!

"You write to communicate to the hearts and minds of others what's burning inside you, and we edit to let the fire show through the smoke."

—*Arthur Plotnik*

Part Four:

After the Writing's done

Fast forward, through the writing process, until... Your book is finished! Congratulations on finishing your book.

Now it's time to take your manuscript to the next phase. Publishing? Nope. It's time to have it edited.

Stay Away From Friends and Family

My best advice to any author is to stay away from friends and family when it comes to editing your manuscript. You may be tempted to ask people close to you to read your book and give you their opinion, but I would recommend against that, as well. Practically speaking, there's simply no need for them to read it until it's done and published in its final form.

Are you ready for some truth? Here it comes.

First off, your good friends and family care about you, so they're not likely to give you an honest assessment of your book. If they don't like it, they may not want to hurt your feelings by telling you the truth so they tell you what you want to hear or at least soften their criticism.

If it's great and they love it, and they tell you so, how can you be sure that's how they really feel?

And what if they *don't* like it and tell you so? It's more likely to sting and bruise our ego if the criticism comes from someone close to us. The reason we ask them in the first place is for validation, to calm our own fears and to try to squelch our self-doubt.

Are you ready for a dose of truth? Here it comes.

The opinions of your friends and loved ones honestly *doesn't matter*. They don't matter at all, in the grand scheme of things. Their opinion isn't a barometer of how successful your book will be. This is especially true if they aren't in your target audience for the book in the first place. Think about it. If you write a science fiction story and your Aunt Mildred loves romance novels but she hates science fiction, would you ask her to read your sci-fi book and give her honest opinion? Um, no. Unless you're a masochist, that is.

Always Hire an Editor

A more practical approach would be to skip the family and friends altogether and hand our work over to a professional editor. And by "professional" I mean someone who gets paid to edit manuscripts.

A professional editor worth their salt will redline the hell out of your manuscript, pointing out spelling and grammatical errors, inconsistencies in voice, and loose ends in the plot you forgot to tie up, and so on.

Be prepared to pay an editor. Even a professional editor who agrees to edit your work for free as a favor isn't likely to give you 100%, if only because they're not getting paid for their time.

Remember, this is their livelihood. If they have to do editing jobs for 6 to 12 hours a day to put food on the table, how much of their time can you expect them to volunteer to professionally edit your manuscript?

Look at it this way: You wouldn't expect an attorney to represent you pro bono, and even if they did you'd know in the back of your mind that they're probably not able (or willing) to give your case as much time and effort as they would if they were getting paid. It's the same with editors.

Getting a free editing pass is a great place to start, but always be willing to pay a professional editor.

What's the Word (Count)?

When it comes to describing your manuscript, start thinking of it in terms of word count; that is, how many total words are in the manuscript. Many people type their book using word processor software, like *Microsoft Word* and describe their books in terms of **page** counts.

"My book is 200 pages long!"

Are you ready for another hard truth? Get ready. Here it comes.

When you describe your manuscript (i.e., your unpublished book) in terms of how many "pages" long it is, two things occur: First, you tell the professionals around you that you're a total amateur and don't know what the hell you're talking about. Second, you impart no real useful information about the length of your book.

You see, an *MS Word* document can be formatted to be 6 x 9 inches in size, or 8.5 x 11 inches. The margins may be a quarter inch all around or two inches around. The font used on the page may be a tiny 6-point Times Roman or a huge 24-point Arial. A 60,000-word manuscript could be 60 pages long or 360 pages long, depending on all of the aforementioned variables.

If I've totally confused you, that's okay. Just know that there are too many variables involved in describing page counts. Printers care about page counts because it defines how much paper they use to print a book.

Editors, on the other hand, care about word counts. The industry standard manuscript "page" is 250 words.

Isn't that much simpler? Let the book designer worry about all that geeky techno stuff. All you need to remember is how many words are in your manuscript. It's easier to remember and in the end, you look smarter. Go figure.

What's the Difference between Copy and Line Editors?

Here are some definitions.

Line Editor: A line editor does a line-by-line review of the manuscript, notes things such as passive voice, wordiness, overused words, and repetitive sentence or paragraph structures. Line editing focuses on the prose itself (e.g., paragraph structure, sentence flow, word choice) rather than on the content in general. Line editors will often use editorial comments and *MS Word's* "track changes" to suggest rewrites to the author.

NOTES

Copy Editor: The copy editor takes raw material to improve the formatting, style, and accuracy of the text. The goal of copy editing is to ensure that content is accurate, easy to follow, fit for its purpose, and free of error, omission, inconsistency, and repetition. In the context of publication in print, copy editing is done before typesetting and again before proofreading, the final step in the editorial cycle.

Within copy editing, there is mechanical editing and substantive editing: *Mechanical editing* is the process of making a text or manuscript follow editorial or house style. The role of this particular type of editing is to keep the preferred style of publication consistent across all content, as well as make sure that generally accepted grammar rules are followed throughout. It refers to editing in terms of spelling, punctuation, correct usage of grammatical symbols, along with reviewing special elements like tables, charts, formatting footnotes, and endnotes. *Substantive editing*, also known as content editing, is the editing of material, including its structure and organization. In this type of editing, internal inconsistencies and discrepancies are dealt with. Substantive editing oftentimes can require heavy editing or rewriting as compared to mechanical editing.

Most copy editors who do electronic editing (e.g., in *MS Word*, rather than marking on a printed copy of the manuscript) will typically mark changes using the "Track Changes" feature.

Note: Before the digital era, copy-editors used to take a red pen to a piece of paper to point out errors and inconsistencies using a markup language made up of symbols universally known by copy-editors. Copy editing symbols can no longer be used when editing digitally because they are not supported on digital platforms such as Track Changes.

Proofreader: The term proofreading is sometimes used to refer to copy-editing, and vice versa. Although there is necessarily some overlap, proofreaders typically lack any real editorial or managerial authority. What they can do is mark queries for typesetters, editors, or authors, provided those queries are few and pointed. Creativity and critical thinking by their very nature conflict with the strict copy-following discipline that commercial and governmental proofreading requires. Thus proofreading and editing are fundamentally separate responsibilities. In contrast, copy editors focus on a sentence-by-sentence analysis of the text to "clean it up" and make it all work together. The copy editor is usually the last editor that an author will work with. Copy editing focuses intensely on style, content, punctuation, grammar, and consistency of usage.

NOTES

How Much Does a Professional Editor Cost?

It's not the cost of hiring an editor that should concern you so much as the cost of *not* hiring one. Imagine the embarrassment of numerous simple mistakes being found in your new book, resulting in terrible reviews, which in turn impact your sales. Simple mistakes that could have been avoided by having your manuscript professionally edited.

The Editorial Freelancers Association (EFA) publishes a chart of common editorial rates (http://the-efa.org/res/rates.php). In this section, I'll give you an idea of what professional editors typically charge. Bear in mind, however, that rates may vary a great deal. Also, when reviewing the below rates, remember that a manuscript "page" is 250 words.

Copy editing: $30-50 per hour. According to the *Writer's Market*, the average is $35. An experienced copy editor might be able to edit roughly 10 pages per hour (PPH). At an hourly rate of $35, they would earn 1.4 cents per word. So the cost to copy edit a 100,000-word manuscript would be $1,400 whereas a 1,000-word children's book would be only $14.

Some copy editors charge a flat rate, such as 2 cents per word. At a flat rate of 2 cents per word, a 100,000-word manuscript would cost $2,000. The same manuscript at a flat rate of a half cent per word would cost $500. According to the *Writer's Market*, the average per-page rate is $4. This works out to $1.280 for an 80,000-word manuscript or $16 for a 1,000-word children's book.

Line editing: $40-60 per hour. At only $40 per hour, an 80,000-word manuscript that took a full two weeks (80 hours) to edit would cost $3,200. Some editors charge only 2 to 3 cents per word. At 3 cents a word, our 100,000-word manuscript would be $3,000 whereas a 1,000-word children's book would be only $30.

Content editing: $45-55 per hour. According to the *Writer's Market*, the average is around $50. Most editors charge around 2 cents to 7½ cents per word, which would run $2,000 to $7,500 for a 100,000-word manuscript, or $20 to $75 for a 1,000-word children's book. According to the *Writer's Market*, the average per-page rate is $7.50. This works out to $3,000 for a 100,000-word manuscript or a $30 for a 1,000-word children's book.

Professional editing costs money, without a doubt. Can you get less expensive editing? Absolutely. As I mentioned before, if you're lucky enough to know an editor who's willing to work cheap, that's an incredible resource. You can also ask your neighbor to edit your manuscript. If they're not a professional editor you may not get very good results. You usually get what you pay for.

Let's look at this example. Cindy has written a book. The manuscript is 80,000 words. Her friend, Tim, is an editor and he agrees to line edit her book for $500. It takes Tim about 60 hours to edit, doing a professional job. At this rate, Tim will be earning about $8.33 an hour to edit Cindy's manuscript. That's actually *below* the minimum wage in many states. As a professional line editor, Tim simply can't make a living at these rates. Tim would be forced to work faster and, as a result, be less thorough editing Cindy's manuscript.

Once again, you get what you pay for.

Another option is to hire someone who's just starting out in the industry and who charges less. Of course, you could also limit yourself to just copy editing, but that won't help you if your plot doesn't work or you need help with point of view issues.

How to Reduce Editing Costs

How much editing costs can vary based on other factors besides the length of the manuscript.

Keep it clean. One way to reduce your editing costs is to turn over to the editor a manuscript that's as clean as possible. Cut out all the unnecessary words and fillers. Correct all the grammar and spelling mistakes you can. Do all of this before sending your manuscript to the editor.

Type of editing: For example, basic copy editing to correct spelling and grammar mistakes costs less than a substantive edit. See the previous section for an explanation of copy editing and substantive editing.

The quality of your writing: The more work the editor has to do to make your manuscript presentable, the more the editing will cost. The fewer mistakes an editor has to find and correct, the faster and smoother the editing process will be. Thus, the faster and less expensive it will be in the end. Good writers submitting a relatively "clean" manuscript pay less. An editor will typically want to see your manuscript (or a sample) before they can quote you a price for editing.

Length: A novel costs more than a short story, naturally. Some editors, however, work on a sliding scale; they charge less per word for a longer manuscript than for a short story.

Editor's experience: An editor who's just starting out and lacks experience may charge you less, but may be of lesser quality than an experienced editor. This depends on the editor, of course. Some "new" editors are quite skilled, but it's a valid consideration nonetheless.

The deadline: If you give your editor a tight deadline, you're almost guaranteed to pay more for the editing. The less flexibility the editor has to move projects around and determine their own schedule, the greater likelihood that they won't be able to fit other jobs into their schedule. Missed work means money lost, so you'll pay them more as a result. Many editors charge a 25% premium for such rush jobs.

Extra read-throughs: If you want the editor to read through your manuscript more than once, you'll likely pay more for the edits. Naturally, it will take longer, as well. It may be worth the money, however, because mistakes often are overlooked on the first read-through, and sometimes the edits introduce new errors to the manuscript.

As you saw above, there are different methods to calculate editing fees. Some editors prefer to charge by the hour. Others offer a flat rate that depends on word count, regardless of how many hours will go into editing the manuscript.

Is It Better to Pay a Flat Rate?

One of the advantages of paying a flat rate is that both the writer and the editor know in advance how much the editing will cost. When paying an hourly rate, you won't know how much the total cost for the job is until the editing is finished.

Some writers worry that an unscrupulous editor will drag out the job in order to have more "billable hours" to beef up their invoice. Does a professional do this? No. Does it happen? It would be naïve to think it never happens. This is where integrity and the editor's experience (and references) come into play.

One disadvantage of paying a flat rate is that it can be difficult to estimate just how much work is involved in editing a manuscript before the editor actually starts working on it. If the editor underestimates the amount of work it will take to get the job done, they will end up working for a very low hourly rate. (Remember, professional editors edit for a living; that means they have to earn enough to live on!)

A Good Editor Makes You Wince

Something I used to tell myself that I now tell my coaching clients is, "If the edits don't make you wince, the editor didn't do their job." By this, I mean that a good editor will find mistakes that make you wince and shake your head.

In the "old days" editors would circle your mistakes in vibrant red ink on your hardcopy manuscript so you couldn't miss them. Nothing humbles an author like getting a "red-lined" manuscript back from the editor! It's human nature not to want to see the mistakes we've made. It can sting the ego.

Amateur writers ignore good editing and they don't learn from it. As a result, they don't get better.

Professional writers learn from their mistakes and become *better* writers. The change is in the doing, however. To get better you must write and you must let others show you your mistakes so you can fix them and improve your craft.

NOTES

"Content precedes design. Design in the absence of content is not design, its decoration."

—*Jeffrey Zeldman*

Part Five:

Book Design

Now that your manuscript is edited and all necessary changes have been made, you're ready to design your book! Book design is also called the "layout" by some folks in the industry. It's designing the look of all the elements that make up the interior of your book: the flow of the text, the number of text columns, the type and size of font used, size and placement of illustrations (if they are used in your book), margin illustrations, page numbers, header and footer elements, and so on.

"What?" you may be saying. "I don't have all that stuff. It's just going to be a novel, like the kind you buy in the grocery store."

Not so. Even the basic "mass market paperback," as they're called, has elements that need to be designed. The type and size of the font used may be pretty standard (such as Times or Times Roman) and there may be no illustrations in your novel, but the placement of page numbers, header elements (such as the title of the book), and the flow of the text must be considered.

It's not that a simple design doesn't require work. It simply requires *less* work.

Should I Hire a Book Designer?

The short answer is, "Yes." A professional book designer will ask you a bunch of questions to understand your vision for what the book should look like. They may make suggestions for improvements but generally you should get a product that looks the way you want it to look.

If your book is a novel or manual of some sort, it should be a relatively straight-forward job. You could get away with not hiring a book designer and do your own layout, for example, but there's a slight learning curve. The last thing you want to do is send files to a printer and have them rejected for any of a number of reasons.

Doing Your Own Book Design

Yes, you can design a basic book in *Microsoft Word*, part of the *Microsoft Office* suite of programs, which also includes *Publisher*. *Office 365* is the current version and will run you as little as $62 for a one-year subscription (or $6.99/month). It's important to consider the final dimensions of your printed book and enter those settings for your document. If you don't know what I'm referring to, you have some learning to do or you should consider hiring a book designer.

For more advanced designs I prefer to use *Adobe InDesign*. Another popular software program for book design is *QuarkXpress*. Both are high-end software programs used in the publishing industry. They are robust and are capable of handling complex designs and outputting files in the precise format required by professional printers.

The downside to these programs is the price. As of the time this book went to print *QuarkXpress* 2016 costs $849 and *InDesign* alone costs $359 for a one-year subscription ($29 a month), or you can lease the whole Adobe *Creative Suite* (CS) of products (including *Photoshop, Illustrator,* and others) for $839.88 a year or $69.99 a month.

There are less expensive alternatives but you will usually sacrifice functionality and flexibility of design when using a less expensive software package.

File Preparation

Fortunately, most of the technical issues involved with file preparation for printers have been made obsolete thanks to Adobe *Acrobat.* I could geek out and spew a bunch of technical mumbo jumbo here. Let me say it simply. Most printers accept books submitted in Acrobat PDF files because PDF files contain everything the printer needs to print the book. (PDF stands for "portable document format." PDF files can be read by any computer using any operating system as long as it has a PDF reader.)

If you are going to do your own layout, you are going to need to learn the basic jargon and some technical stuff. There's no way around it. Otherwise, you'll need to have someone do it for you (and likely pay them). Luckily, most printers now provide all of the information you need to properly convert your book design files to a PDF file for the printer.

Nowadays it can be as simple as "printing" your *Word* document. Instead of printing it to your inkjet printer on the desk, however, you select "Print to PDF"

Book Design Resources

Acrobat Pro:
https://acrobat.adobe.com/us/en/acrobat/acrobat-pro-cc.html

Acrobat Reader (Free): https://get.adobe.com/reader/

InDesign: http://www.adobe.com/products/indesign.html

LibreOffice: http://www.libreoffice.org/

Microsoft Office: http://www.microsoftstore.com/Office

QuarkXpress: http://www.quark.com

NOTES

"I strive for two things in design: simplicity and clarity. Great design is born of those two things."

—*Lindon Leader*

Part Six:

Cover Design

Your book's cover is arguably the single most important part of the book when it comes to sales. Imagine someone walking down an aisle at the bookstore, browsing the selection of books. What stands out? The books with the attractive covers. If someone is looking for a specific title or author, they may examine the text on the spines of books. Otherwise, it's generally the cover that first grabs the eye. You can use a plain color, a photo, a painting, or something else for your cover.

It's All about Feeling

Here's a rule of human nature and sales. People buy based on emotion, then they justify their purchase with facts. When we buy a new car, it's ultimately got nothing to do with the MPG or safety rating. It's how the car makes us *feel* when we're driving it. That other stuff just solidifies our intention to buy it.

A cover needn't be super flashy to be attractive. When designing a book cover, the idea is to put an image on the cover that will conjure in a buyer's mind an emotion or desire.

Consider romance novels. Of course they use hunky, shirtless male models and beautiful female models with pouty lips, long flowing hair and cleavage showing for illustrations on their covers. Think about their audience. Who's buying the books?

Sometimes Less Is More

A simple image, such as a symbol, can achieve that goal as well as a complex painting or illustration, sometimes better. Look at the covers of books in the *Twilight* or *Hunger Games* series, or almost any Stephen King book. In my own book (shameless self-promotion here), *Semicolon; Memoir of a Colon Cancer Survivor*, I used a photograph of myself, a huge semicolon symbol, and a descriptive title.

This is a web page with 50 great book cover designs on it. Check it out for some inspiration: http://bit.ly/cool-covers

Hardcover or Paperback?

The design of your cover will be a little different depending on whether it's a paperback or hardcover.

Whether you produce your book as a paperback or a hardcover will ultimately come down to price. If you're willing to spend a few extra dollars to produce *each copy* of your book, you can publish your book as a hardcover. You'll need to increase the retail price of your book by about twice that amount to cover that extra production cost, however. If that doesn't make sense for your project, then stick with a paperback.

Paperback: Paperbacks, also called softcovers, are books with a cardstock cover. In the printing industry, the material is usually referred to as 10-point or 10pt, referring to the thickness of the stock. The cover is glued to the book (called "perfect binding"). Paperbacks usually have a cover image, as well as text on the spine and back cover (sometimes art is also on the back).

Paperbacks are much less expensive to produce than hardcovers but aren't as durable. Because of the cost difference, most books are released as paperbacks.

Hardcover: Hardcovers, also called hardbacks, are books sewn to a chipboard cover (called "case binding") that's laminated with printed material or some other material, such as cloth, vinyl, leather, etc. If the non-printed material is used, the cover may include the title of the book stamped on it with ink or metallic foil.

So-called "cloth" hardcovers will often have what's called a "dust jacket" on it, which is nothing more than a book cover made of a sheet of printed (and sometimes coated) paper stock that wraps around the cover, front and back. The inside flaps of the dust jacket may include text about the book or author, as well as the ISBN and price of the book (more on these later).

Inside the covers are "endpapers," sheets that help secure the collective pages to the cover. Traditionally they were plain but today they may include text, or include artwork.

"The difference between something good and something great is attention to detail."

—*Charles R. Swindoll*

Part Seven:
Don't Forget the ISBN

What's an ISBN?

ISBN stands for International Standards Book Number. Up to the end of 2006, ISBNs were 10 digits in length. Since January 1, 2007, however, ISBNs now consist of 13 digits. ISBNs are calculated using a specific mathematical formula and include a check digit to validate the number.

An ISBN is essentially a product identifier used by publishers, booksellers, libraries, internet retailers and other supply chain participants for ordering, listing, sales records and stock control purposes. The ISBN identifies the registrant as well as the specific title, edition, and format (*source: International ISBN Agency*).

There is a great FAQ page on the International ISBN Agency website, at https://www.isbn-international.org/content/what-isbn.

Do I Have to Have an ISBN?

No. But you'll want to have one for your book. ISBNs are the way bookstores know how to find and order your book. Unless you're going to sell your book out of the trunk of your car at the flea market every weekend, you're going to need an ISBN.

Each separate edition or version of a book must have a unique ISBN. For example, you publish a hardcover book. Later you release it in paperback, then as an eBook. Later you make a few changes and release a new edition. You would need a separate ISBN for each edition (one for the hardcover, one for each edition of the paperback, and one for the eBook edition).

How Do I Get an ISBN?

R. R. Bowker is the official ISBN Agency for the United States and its territories. They are the sole source for ISBNs for publishers in the United States.

Currently, a single ISBN costs $125, a block of 10 will cost you $250, you can buy a block of 100 for $575, or (for the truly prolific publisher) you can buy a block of 1,000 for $1,500. To order one or more ISBNs, go to http://bit.ly/buy-ISBN.

Bowker also runs a website with resources for self-published authors, at http://www.selfpublishedauthor.com.

How Do I Get an ISBN Barcode?

There are a number of third-party sellers of ISBN barcodes. You aren't required to use any particular one. You could use a service, buy software to make your own. I print my books through *LightningSource*, which creates a barcode for you.

There is a great list of Frequently Asked Questions about ISBN barcodes here: http://bit.ly/ISBN-barcode-FAQ.

"There is more treasure in books than in all the pirate's loot on Treasure Island."

—*Walt Disney*

Part Eight:
Printing Your Book

Your manuscript is all edited. You've received all of the art you commissioned for the cover and interior. Your interior book design is finished and your book is all laid out. You're finally ready to go to print!

What do you do now?

Which Format Should I Produce: eBook or Print?

The first step is to determine how you're going to produce and distribute your book. Are you producing an eBook version, a print edition, or both?

For the record, I always suggest both. Here's why. As I mentioned earlier in this book, even if you would prefer to see your book in printed format over an electronic edition, you'd be well advised to consider releasing an electronic format as well. If your paperback sells 10,000 copies but an additional 5,000 people would rather buy a copy only if it were available on *Kindle* and other devices, why ignore those additional sales?

It's silly to ignore potential sales when the effort to release an eBook edition is barely more than simply producing a print edition. The manuscript's already written and edited, and the basic book is designed. It could be literally a few extra clicks of the mouse to generate an eBook version of your book and open the door to an additional potential revenue stream.

Traditional Printing or POD?

Traditionally, books were only printed using a large offset press printing machine. The cost for printing books was quite high. Printing a run of 5,000 copies of a book could cost thousands of dollars. The cost per copy was lower for larger print runs, but low print runs (less than 1,000 books) just weren't practical.

Along came POD. POD stands for **Print on Demand**. With POD, publishers can now produce as few as one or two books at a time, allowing them to fill very small orders. The price per copy is much higher than with large runs on a traditional press, but still low enough that a publisher can enjoy a small profit on even sales of a single copy. This meant that event books long since out of print could be "revived" and offered for sale.

There are a number of companies offering POD service. For the most part, most POD printers will print however many copies of your book that you want and ship them to you. For my money, I prefer services that also act as a conduit to sales outlets. The goal, after all, is to make your book available for sale, not to stack them in your closet where no one will see them.

Print on Demand Companies

Over the years a number of POD companies have come and gone. Several big players remain. Those are the ones I will cover in this book. A smaller company may be more to your liking and that's okay. For my money, however, I prefer full service.

LightningSource: *LightningSource* (LS) is owned by Ingram Books, arguably the world's largest book distribution company.

When you register an account with *LightningSource*, you become part of "the system." When you upload your book files and metadata (book information) a few weeks or more ahead of the "release date," you have the option of listing your book in Ingram's "coming soon" catalog of books.

Regardless when you upload the files, your book will automatically be available from Amazon.com and other retail outlets. Any copies bought will be fulfilled by *LightningSource*. As the publisher, you earn the wholesale price of the book (i.e., the price retailers pay LS, about 45% of the retail price). LS subtracts the production cost of the copies it printed and shipped. The rest is yours.

LightningSource is excellent about tracking sales and royalties, with monthly reports being sent to you. For more information, go to http://lightningsource.com

IngramSpark: *IngramSpark* (IS) is also owned by Ingram Books. Like LightningSource, it uses POD technology to produce small to medium runs of books and offers distribution to a huge network of booksellers, both online and traditional bookstores.

IngramSpark is essentially a streamlined version of LS, designed for the self-publishing author, as it presumably uses the same facilities, equipment, and distribution channels as LS.

For more information, go to http://www.ingramspark.com.

CreateSpace: Then there is *CreateSpace* (CS), an Amazon.com company (formerly *BookSurge*). While CS can be used for producing and selling books, audio CDs, and even DVDs, I'll be discussing only the book side of the business.

You can register a *CreateSpace* account for free. *CreateSpace* includes various distribution options. Your book can be made available from Amazon.com and other retail outlets. You can opt to have your book available through "expanded distribution channels" (meaning other book sellers). The latter option can take six weeks to begin once you opt for it.

CreateSpace also has a suite of free tools to help you create your book, for those who don't do their own book design or hire someone to do it for them. In addition, CS will generate an ISBN and barcode for you if you don't have one.

Like *LightningSource*, CS pays you a royalty equal to the wholesale price of your book (40% of your book's US list price online; rates for other countries may differ), minus the bookseller's "share" (the production cost plus an additional flat fee). Unlike *LightningSource*, there's no cost for uploading files (covers and interior pages) for each book.

For more information, go to https://www.createspace.com.

Lulu: *Lulu* is one of the larger POD book printers, and claims to have the largest online distribution. *Lulu* has an attractive and easy-to-use online interface for determining the cost of producing your book. Like the other services, *Lulu* pays authors a royalty based on the wholesale cost (generally one-half of the retail price), minus the production cost and *Lulu's* commission.

Print and eBooks can be published and offered for sale in the Lulu Marketplace at no cost. Lulu also offers a free *globalREACH* distribution for print and eBooks, essentially making your book available for order from retailers. It requires your book to have an ISBN, which Lulu is able to sell you if you haven't already acquired one.

For information go to https://www.lulu.com.

Other Companies: There are other POD printing companies out there, as an online search would quickly show. In my opinion, the above four are the biggest players in the POD space and the ones most worthy of consideration.

For many years, my company of choice was Ingram's *LightningSource*. I was familiar with the publishing and printing process so it was a simple matter for me to properly format files, upload them for a project, pay the fee, and have my books available from Amazon.com and other retail outlets. Getting my books set up, printed, and into distribution channels was a snap. I've been a LS client for nearly two decades.

Today, however, things are different. In my opinion, the overall winner – and my company of choice for POD and distribution – is *CreateSpace*. With a slightly higher royalty percentage on sales, no-cost uploading of book files, free online tools, and the speed with which books are made available for sale online, the "one stop shopping" that CreateSpace offers is phenomenal.

NOTES

POD Production Cost & Royalty Price Comparisons

The following price comparison assumes a single copy of a book available from Amazon.com and other retail outlets, with the following specifications: Paperback, 6x9", perfect bound, full-color C1S 10-pt cover (or equivalent), B&W printing, white 40# paper, 120 pages, and a retail price of $14.95.

	LightningSource	IngramSpark	CreateSpace	Lulu
Retail Price	$14.99	$14.99	$14.99	$14.99
Wholesale	$6.75	$6.75	N/A	$7.48
Manuf.	$2.67	$2.67	$2.29	$5.50
Fee	$0.00	$0.00	$0.80	$0.40
Royalty	$4.08	$4.08	$6.70	$1.58

NOTES

"If the book is true, it will find an audience that is meant to read it."

—*Wally Lamb*

Part Nine:
Marketing Your Book

The doorbell rings. You vibrate with excitement as you bound toward the door. It's the parcel delivery person with a box of your brand new books! Your grab the box and run inside, tearing open the box. There they are, in all their splendor, stacked in two neat rows. The cover is so shiny! (Inhaling deeply) Ah, that new book smell. It's like a dream come true! As you revel in the magical feeling of being a real published author with real printed books to show for your efforts, a sudden feeling of dread befalls you. Oh, no! You've done so much work to get to this point but how will people know about your new book? Who's going to buy it? After a book is published the real work begins.

"What?" you may be thinking. "Writing, editing, book design, and printing aren't real work?"

Well, yes, they are. But now that you have a book to sell you must market it.

Finding People Who Care

Nobody cares about your new book. Well, not unless they know about it first, that is. The trick is to help people learn about your book so you can find the ones who care, or at least care enough to consider buying your book.

So what are some economic ways to market your new book?

The Landscape of Marketing Today

More than 70% of internet views of web pages or social media is accomplished on a smartphone. What does that say about the direction we're going as a society? It says social media is the *defacto* way for companies and brands to interact with consumers and the way those consumers are connecting is with their cell phone. Keep this in mind as you're marketing your book.

Paid Advertising

The last thing I recommend a self-published author do is pay for advertising. There are simply too many other ways to market your book that cost little to no money. With that said, paid advertising is still something you can do fairly inexpensively. Here are the places I have used to promote my books and other products.

Facebook: *Facebook* still has one of the best ROI (Return On Investment) venues in the advertising space. You can target your advertising, unlike any other advertising venue, using incredible demographics and personal interests. Think about it. Where else can you spend $10 and reach 3,000 to 5,000 with a direct interest in what you're promoting? If your book is a murder mystery, buy an ad targeting 3-5,000 readers of mystery books. If you wrote a health and wellness book, buy an ad targeting 3-5,000 people who have purchased health and wellness products in the last year.

With *Facebook Ads Manager* you can promote an advertisement you create, do split ads using different images and/or text, promote a *Facebook* Page or an individual post, driving traffic to your Page or to a website. There are many options. I find the ads manager tools to be somewhat clunky but (in my humble opinion) still easier to use than some others.

Oh, and *Facebook* has 1.59 billion active users.

Instagram: Instagram began allowing paid advertising on its service, which is no surprise as it was acquired by *Facebook*. With a reported 400,000,000 active users, Instagram is a social media platform you should be looking at.

Twitter Ads: "Twitter?" you might be thinking. "Really?" Absolutely. Twitter is possibly the largest social media platform out there. With a sufficiently appealing piece of media content (an image or a short video) promoting your book, you can promote that tweet and use hashtags to help target viewers who are interested in what you're writing about. Unlike most other social media platforms, Twitter allows its 320,000,000 active users to directly interact with each other. That's powerful.

Should I Have a Presence on Social Media?

In 2016, Statista.com ranked the following social networks by number of users. The results are eye-opening.

- *Facebook*: 1,590,000,000 active users
- *Tumblr*: 555,000,000 active users
- *Instagram*: 400,000,000 active users
- *Twitter*: 320,000,000 active users
- *Snapchat*: 200,000,000 active users
- *Pinterest*: 100,000,000 active users
- *LinkedIn*: 100,000,000 active users

If, after seeing those numbers, you don't see the value of having a presence on social media, you need a kick in the ass.

If – I mean, *when* – you decide to have a presence on social media, pick your platforms and learn the rules. What I mean is, you need to understand how that platform works, how users interact, and how you get attention and can organically (i.e., naturally, without sending money) gain traffic and followers on that platform.

If you pick only three social media platforms to participate on, I recommend *Facebook*, *Twitter*, and *Instagram*.

Third Party Social Media Tools

I also recommend using a tool that allows you to post to those accounts remotely. Here are a few popular tools that I use.

Hootsuite: *Hootsuite* offers a free account with which you can manage multiple streams for up to three different platforms. For example, you can have one section for your *Facebook* Page (with feeds for your posts, scheduled posts, and fan posts), another section for your *Twitter* account (with feeds for your tweets, your mentions, retweets, etc.), and a third for your *Instagram* account.

There are paid accounts allowing unlimited social media accounts to be managed, for those with a social media budget. I don't recommend a paid account for people starting out. There is also a *Hootsuite* phone app, to allow you to manage your account on the go.

For information, go to http://hootsuite.com

TweetJukebox: *TweetJukebox* is a scheduling service that allows you to create a "jukebox" that contains tweets you compose and schedule for posting, much the way a classic jukebox holds 45 records. These tweets don't disappear, however. They are recycled and rotated and can be tweeted again later, at intervals you set.

TweetJukebox offers a free account that allows up to two "jukeboxes" with a total of up to 300 tweets, and limited options. Paid accounts are also offered with additional features, such as the ability to upload a list of tweets (instead of adding them one at a time with a free account).

For information, go to http://tweetjukebox.com

Other Apps: There are other apps available, including those that will track new users, users who stop following you, some that will automatically send a message to new followers, and some that do all of the above.

These functions sound handy but bear in mind that different social media platforms have Terms of Service (TOS) that prohibit certain automated activity. Use of these apps could potentially cause you to violate the rules, jeopardizing the good standing of your account. Be careful what you use and make sure its use doesn't violate the rules of the platforms you're using them on.

NOTES

There are plenty of ways to grow your audience that cost you nothing but time. Here are a few of the most effective strategies.

Host a blog: This is such an important topic, I've given it its own section, below. If you only read one section of this book, this is it. Seriously. When you get to it, use a highlighter, scribble notes in the margins, do whatever you need to do to absorb as much of the info as you can.

Use Social Media: This is another biggie, which I covered earlier in this chapter. If you haven't read it, go back and do so. In fact, if you only read one part of this book, this should be it.

Participate in Online Communities: There are online communities built around nearly every topic imaginable. Find ones that are built around the topic you wrote about. It's easier than ever to find *Facebook* Groups, find *Twitter* Lists or other online forums where people meet virtually to discuss various topics. Find and join a few of these groups.

Get to know the people, the forum rules, and the posting etiquette before you start posting. Some forums have strict rules about posting "commercial" or solicitous messages, or messages of any kind containing links. It's good practice to create and nurture relationships with the other users. Let them get to know and develop a trust for you. You want to be known as someone who participates and adds value to the community, rather than be seen as an outsider who's come only to spam them with requests to buy your book. Does it take time? Yes, but it's worth it.

Business Cards: Business cards are a great source of exposure. They are inexpensive and make great handouts that convey a professional image. Here are some things to consider when creating your business card.

Make the card about you, not about your book. Use a professional-looking headshot of yourself. If you include a picture a book, include it in addition to, not instead of, your face. Include the contact info you want to give to strangers. If that means only a website address, then that's okay. Include social media icons but only include the URL (i.e., web address) of your website. Your goal is always to drive traffic to your website.

Pay a little extra and use the back of the card to include a generic image – such as a sunset or waving flag – and a "Thank You!" message. This turns your marketing material into something more memorable.

Take a Class: For starters, you'll learn something. I suggest taking a class related to your new status as a published author or related to the topic you wrote about. You will learn more, contributing to your status as a subject matter expert. In addition, you may be able to use your book or personal experiences as the subject of class assignments. And let's not forget, you'll also be talking to and possibly socializing with other students in your class over the course of the semester, right? Not only do they have an interest in what you're doing or what you wrote about, but what always comes up? "What do you do?"

Host a Class: This is even better for establishing yourself as an authority in your field. Even if you *don't* have a teaching credential to teach a college course, you can be an instructor in parks and recs class or in a continuing education course through your local school district. Imagine speaking to 20 or 30 or even 50 people, all of whom want to learn about a topic you published a book on!

It's not a good idea (nor ethical) to hang a poster promoting your book in every class session, but you *can* mention being a published author when you introduce yourself. In addition, at the *end* of the class, it's certainly appropriate to mention your book as a resource for additional information.

Even if you just list your contact information (including your website address), that will drive additional pre-qualified traffic to your website, which is likely to convert to new followers and, ultimately, readers.

Public Speaking: Hosting a class will give you speaking experience in front of small groups. If you can build up some courage, you can take speaking to the next level and start speaking to larger groups, such as corporate events, church groups, or *MeetUp* groups, about your topic of choice. Even if you speak for free (as many speakers do starting out) the host will typically allow you to have a table from which to sign – and sell – your books before and after the event.

Guest Blogging: You host a blog, right? Of course, you do. So why not offer to write a blog post or short article about your favorite topic for *another* blog? Many bloggers welcome the extra content and the added value it provides their readers. It also provides you exposure to many potential new fans, who may go to your own blog for more of that awesome content you're giving away.

Freelance Articles: Writing freelance article for publications or websites can be a huge boon to gaining new fans and readers. Some sites pay their freelance authors but those gigs are harder to come by. Even an unpaid guest article can be gold for an author because most publications print a "byline," listing the submitter's name and a credit (such as the name of their latest book). Some even allow a short bio at the end of the article, with a link to the author's website. A single short article on the Huffington Post could drive tens of thousands of new readers to your website or to your book on sellers' websites.

Use Your E-mail: Every e-mail is a potential advertisement for you, and it isn't considered spam. The secret is in your e-mail signature. A signature is a block of text that is auto-inserted in every e-mail you compose. It normally contains your name, if nothing else, but it can also contain the title of your book with a link to the listing on an online store, or to your website.

To generate a signature block for Gmail, click on the gear icon in the upper right of the window, near your name and image. Then click "Settings," and scroll down until you see the setting for "Signature."

Here's what my signature looks like.

Sincerely,

Mark T. Arsenault
Author, Coach, Teacher, Actor & Entrepreneur
http://MarkTruth.com

It's nothing fancy. It doesn't need to be. It clearly and simply communicates who I am, what I do, and how people can get more information about me.

Book Signings: If you're thinking you can't do a book signing because book signings are only for celebrities, think again. If you're a published author, you're a local celebrity, at least as far as everyone else knows.

Contact your local bookstore(s) and talk to the manager. Ask to schedule a book signing and offer to bring a small supply of your books the store can purchase (at wholesale) for the fans who don't already own a copy. It's a no-risk venture for the store and has a huge upside for you. The bookstore will likely promote the event in its newsletter. You, in turn, can promote it on your blog and on social media. Develop some synergy.

Once you've done a local signing, try contacting a bookstore in a neighboring town. Going out of state on business or vacation in a few months? Contact a bookstore in the area you're traveling to... Now you're an author who's "flying in for a book signing."

Press Releases: This topic deserves a bit more space, so I've given it its own section, below.

Create a Trailer: You've seen those 30-second to 2-minute-long videos promoting a movie, right? Those are called "trailers." You can create a trailer for your book. And you should create one. Why? Because *YouTube* is the second largest site used for searching, period. Millions of people are using smartphones and flat screen TVs to watch *YouTube* videos. Trust me. Create a trailer for your book.

There's no reason to spend the big money for a professional video editing program when something as basic (not to mention free) as *iMovie* or *Windows MovieMaker* can do the trick. There are also a number of websites that provide a simple interface to let users make short videos. You can upload a few pictures, type some text, and even add royalty-free music, to create a professional-looking trailer for your book. Websites such as Animoto.com, Kizoa.com, and Shakr.com can all do the trick.

Personal Development: Jim Rohn said, "For things to get better, you have to get better." That applies to attraction marketing as much as it does every other aspect of your life.

Investing time and money into personal development has a better return than any other single form of investment. It's been said that for every dollar you invest in yourself it returns $30 down the road, in terms of financial success and abundance.

Even the Bible tells us "Do not be conformed to this world, but be transformed by the renewal of your mind... (Rom. 12:2) "to be made new in the attitude of your minds." (Eph. 4:23)

I recommend reading at least 30 minutes – or 10 pages – a day from a personal development book (or video). Anything that renews your positive outlook, lifts your spirit and boosts your confidence. It will make a huge difference to your future, I assure you. In the words of my friend and mentor, John C. Maxwell, "Change is inevitable. Growth is optional." Be intentional about your growth.

Press Releases

Writing a press release is an art form. There are a number of free resources from which to learn the art. There are also a number of fee-based resources that you can use to have someone draft your press release for you.

What to include: Your press release needs to include information about your book, about you and how to contact you. There are a ton of websites dedicated to helping people craft a good press release, including what to include in it, how to format it, and so on, so I won't go into any more detail about it here. In fact, a quick search on *Google* for "how to create a press release" returned more than 130 *million* results.

Make it Newsworthy: The trick to writing a good press release is to provide all of the information in a way that is interesting and "newsworthy" to the end recipient. Too many press releases are written like this:

"Awesome book was just released. It's written by Miss Smarty, who has a Shiny Award. Awesome book is about this topic. Awesome book is available at all the usual retailers. Contact info. Blah, blah, blah."

Ready for some hard truth? Nobody in the newsroom cares. That kind of press release is very unlikely to get printed in a newspaper. So how do you make a press release appealing to editors? Make it "newsworthy." You need to tie the dry information to something of interest to the reporters and editors. Make it timely. Make it related to something important, controversial, or otherwise interesting in the news world. Here's an example:

"Shiny Award-winning local author, Miss Smarty, is the featured guest at this month's Bookstore event. Miss Smarty will be signing copies of her latest book, Awesome book, which hits store shelves this month. "I'm very excited to be back in Localtown for this book signing," said Smarty. Contact info."

See the difference? So will the editor. Help the news outlets by writing an interesting story *for* them and they'll be more likely to publish your press release, perhaps verbatim.

Distribution: Once your press release is done, who do you send it to? If you're going to do your own press release distribution (presumably to save money), you'll need to start collecting a list of places to send them to. Go for e-mail addresses or web pages used for submitting press releases. Don't forget to post the press release on your blog and on social media platforms!

Let's face the hard truth, here. It's going to take hours upon hours to collect a lot of contacts yourself. Fortunately, there are press release distributing companies which, for a fee, can get your press release delivered to literally tens of thousands of news outlets. They can even filter them by topic, geographical region, and a number of other categories. And most press release distribution sites also have a bunch of free resources to help you learn to craft an effective press release. If you have the money and inclination to pay for press release distribution, two of the better-known distributors are Newswire.com and prweb.com.

Why Should I Host a Blog?

Believe it or not, creating a blog is one of the most common things that successful entrepreneurs attribute their success to. Blogging is arguably the single most effective means of "attraction marketing," outside of *YouTube* (which is itself a critical piece of the blogging puzzle).

A number of hugely successful entrepreneurs, like business builder and branding expert Gary Vaynerchuk to network marketing advocates and trainers Eric Worre and Ray Higdon, attribute the growth of their audience – and subsequently their brands – to blogging.

There are people today receiving literally thousands of leads a month from efforts they put into their blogs months or even years ago. Let that sink in for a minute or two. How many people have you talked to about your book in the last month? Imagine having 5,000 new potential buyers discover your book each and every month, on autopilot.

Hosting a blog sounds pretty intriguing now, I bet, doesn't it?

So how do you create an effective blog that will attract leads? There are entire training courses around building and maintaining a blog to build an audience and gain leads. Some cost hundreds of dollars but are worth every penny for those who are serious about building brand equity and making money from their blogging.

Here are a few basic things you should know about blogging.

Web Hosting: You'll need to find a company to lease you server space to host the files that make up your website. There are a number of companies that provide inexpensive web hosting. If you're not planning to handle the website creation and file management yourself, you'll need to hire someone to do it for you. Fortunately, *Wordpress* is fairly easy to install and makes website creation as simple as picking elements and clicking your mouse. In fact, you can even register on Wordpress.com and have *them* host your website and blog!

Domain Name: You'll need to register a domain name that will point folks to your web page. It will cost about $15 a year but you can often get the first year at crazy discounts from places like 1and1.com, GoDaddy.com, and other registrars. Try to choose a name that both conveys your brand and is easy to remember. DenverBirthdayClown.com is a lot better than Mike-the-Denver-Birthday-clown-555-1212.com! Even though the latter may be better in terms of SEO, the first one is overall a much better choice of domain names.

Give Content Away: If you haven't heard this before, know that giving away free content is the key to gaining followers and being successful as an entrepreneur. It may seem counterintuitive. After all, if you give stuff away for free, why would anyone pay you for your stuff? Get ready for another hard truth.

People will only do business with you if they know, like and trust you. You are not Scholastic or Simon & Schuster, with the long-term built up brand equity and customer loyalty that those names possess. You are you. So the way to let people get to know you and your product, to find the ones who like you, and to ultimately gain their trust, you add value to people and to the community they are a part of.

The free content can be a blog post, a video commentary on *YouTube*, your quote on *Twitter*, a How-to article on your website, an infographic on *Instagram* or *Tumblr*, or any number of things you put out there that are interesting, informative or entertaining.

Gary Vaynerchuk, the author of *Jab, Jab, Jab, Right Hook: How to Tell Your Story in a Noisy Social World*, said it well when he said, "Jabs are the lightweight pieces of content that benefit your customers by making them laugh, snicker, ponder, play a game, feel appreciated, or escape; right hooks are calls to action that benefit your businesses."

Learn SEO: SEO stands for "search engine optimization." Simply put, it's knowing how to select web page titles, create content, use keywords, use pictures, and all that jazz, to get your web page or (YouTube video) to rank high on search engines. It's a big topic and I don't expect the average person to get it all in just a couple hours of research. But you should be at least aware of a few basic things that will help your page's SEO.

Try to include keywords in your page title and throughout your blog or article. Try to choose a keyword(s) that aren't super popular because your page will never beat out the thousands of others on search returns. Try to select less popular keywords that are still relevant to your content. For example, "bowling" is probably a super popular keyword, returning 197 million results. Way down on page 20 is a listing for an archived web page titled *Thursday Night Social Bowling League - San Jose*. Now, if

I do a Google search for "Social Bowling League" guess which page pops up as the third, fourth *and* fifth listings on page one of the search results. That's the power of using keywords effectively.

Other SEO tips include making sure your web page loads quickly, adding keywords to the "alt text" tags of pictures used on the page, having at least 300 words in your blog post, and avoiding run-on sentences. There are too many other tips to mention. SEO is a specialty in and of itself.

If you're running your own website, start learning SEO. If you're using WordPress on your site, consider getting an SEO plug-in. If you have someone doing the design and upkeep for you, ask them about SEO. If they're worth their salt they'll be happy to tell you what they're doing to help your site rank in searches.

Post consistently: A blog where someone posts once or twice a month, on random days, isn't appealing to fans nor to search indexing bots. Sporadic posting won't attract readers, as well as a blog with new content, posted every day, like clockwork. Human beings are creatures of habit. They like to know that things they like are going to be there consistently. If you promise a new video every week, post a new video every week. If you say you're going to post new content twice a day, 365 days a year, then you better post new content twice a day, 365 days a year.

More frequent new content is better because you'll more quickly collect a library of material, which (if created properly) will continue to attract readers indefinitely; what's called a piece of "evergreen" content. But it's better to post one piece of content every week, on schedule, than sporadically post things with no set schedule.

Incorporate social media: Readers should be able to comment and share your blog, whether it's the whole site or a specific post, with their friends on social media. Having "like" and "share" buttons for the various popular social media platforms will only help expand the range of readership.

For example, I replaced the standard comment feature on my blog with a Facebook comment box, using a plug-in. With 1.5 billion active users, it's a safe bet that most of my readers are using Facebook. If they comment on my blog and also share that comment on their own FB wall, using the handy check box, then they've just shared my page with their Friends.

Use consistent branding: Start thinking in terms of "cross-platform branding." What online username do you use for yourself, your book or your business? Whatever it is, think long term and cross-platform. You want a name that you can use consistently across the various social media platforms that you plan to be active on.

I suggest using your actual face for your profile photo instead of just a logo. It's easier for people to relate to a face than a company logo. Of course, you could always incorporate your logo into the image. Your background or "wall" image should be the same basic image on every platform, too. You'll need to create images of the size recommended for each platform, but the goal is consistency. When people go from your *Facebook* business page to your website then to your *Twitter* account, they should immediately know they are interacting with the same entity.

For example, let's say Amy Jones is writing a book called *Firescape* and self-published it under the imprint AJ Publishing. Her online name in social media could be "Amy Jones," she could use "AJ Publishing" or she could use the name of her book or a variant, such as "Firescape_book." She starts creating a Facebook page and decides to use "AJ Publishing." Then she creates a Twitter account and uses the same basic name for her Twitter handle ("AJPublishing"). She's lucky and the name is also available on Instagram and *Google+/YouTube!*

Repurpose Content: A number of people who teach branding and entrepreneurship say that posting content daily on your blog is the single most powerful thing you can do to grow your brand and your business. There's a way you can post not just content to your blog but you can also use that same content to post additional content to social media platforms to help drive traffic to your blog. That is by repurposing content.

Here's an example. If you shoot and upload a two-minute video about a subject you're passionate about, you can then transcribe that video and post the text with the video in your blog. Now you have two pieces of content: text and video. You can also extract the audio from your video and post that to *Soundcloud* or *iTunes* as a podcast. You can take a single frame (a still image) from your video, overlay a quote from that same video along with the URL to your blog. Voila! You have now a graphic to post on Instagram.

You can turn one piece of work into so many pieces of content across different social media platforms that you can effectively put out a dozen pieces of content a day. That is one way to gain a following, pulling from different platforms and directing them to your blog and your mailing list because that's where the money is.

Engage with your audience: Don't just post content and think that's all there is to do. Don't just walk away from that platform until the next time you post something. Engage with the people who interact with your content. Talk to them. It's a courtesy, it takes you a second, and it shows gratitude. People like that. Start building the relationship with your followers.

If you're on Twitter and someone retweets something you tweeted, post a thank you. Something like "@followerguy Thank you for the RT!" Look at what they're posting and if you like something, tell them. If someone likes your latest post on your Facebook page, send them a private message to say, "I saw you gave my latest post a 'Like.' Thanks. I really appreciate it."

As Gary Vaynerchuk says, "Continue the conversation." It's the way to build a following of real people who get to know you, like you, and eventually promote you or your next project to *their* friends and followers. Instead of working hard to promote to 1,000 contacts, you have 1,000 *other* people working to promote to *their* 1,000 contacts. Why would you want to keep working hard to promote to a few thousand people when you can work hard to build relationships and eventually have other people promote to a million people? That's the power of social media.

NOTES

NOTES

"The copyright bargain: a balance between protection for the artist and rights for the consumer."

—*Robin Gross*

Part Ten:

Copyrights and Trademarks

Few topics are more misunderstood and spark more conversation among authors and would-be authors than these.

In the mid-'90s, when I first considered publishing, I was in a conversation with a group of experienced publishers. I made an ignorant comment (perhaps naïve is a more appropriate adjective). In it I confused copyrights and trademarks. A common mistake among lay people, but in my prospective peer group it was laughable. And laugh they did. I was quickly corrected, followed by a smiles and consolatory pat on the back.

I never forgot that experience. I realized I had a lot to learn about intellectual property (IP) laws and, if I planned on becoming a publisher, I needed to learn them ASAP.

What follows is the basic information you'll need to hold your own in a conversation about copyrights and trademarks.

Understand a few things, however.

First, this chapter applies to U.S. copyright law. If you're in another jurisdiction, this doesn't necessarily apply to you (unless you're publishing a work in the U.S.).

Second, nothing in this book should be considered legal advice. If, for any reason, you believe you may be heading for – or are in the midst of – litigation involving copyrights (or anything else, for that matter) put down this book and consult an attorney! Are you ready for some more hard truth? I am not an attorney, nor have I ever played one on television.

What is copyright?

According to the U.S. Copyright Office, "Copyright is a form of protection granted by law for original works of authorship fixed in a tangible medium of expression." Blah, blah, blah. What does that all really mean?

The word "copyright" is a compound word. If you split it into two words you get the meaning. "Copyright" is essentially the *right* to make *copies*. Whoa! Did you see that? (You'll note the word is *not* spelled "copywrite." Don't be a noob. Always spell it correctly.)

If you own the rights to the work (i.e., the copyright) then you have the legal right to make copies of that work and give them away (or sell them).

What does copyright protect?

Copyright...protects original works of authorship including literary, dramatic, musical, and artistic works, such as poetry, novels, movies, songs, computer software, and architecture (source: copyright.gov).

Basically, it can be a written work (such as a story, an article, a biography, a poem, song notes and/or lyrics, etc.), auditory (such as a musical or spoken performance), a physical work (such as a sculpture or painting), or purely visual (such as a
74

motion picture). Anything you create and "express" through some tangible and perceivable form can be protected.

Copyright does not protect facts, ideas, systems, or methods of operation, although it may protect the way these things are expressed (source: copyright.gov).

Copyright protect example

To illustrate what is and isn't protected by copyright let's take a motion picture and break down the different elements.

First there is the idea for the story. Let's say it's a fantastic story idea. The best ever. Can an idea be protected by copyright? No, it can't! Why? Because it hasn't been expressed in a tangible form. It's a good thing it can't be protected, too. Ideas are a dime a dozen. I get at least $1.20 worth of ideas each and every day. Some are good, some are mediocre, and some are just lame. But none of them can be protected by copyright until I somehow *express* them in tangible form.

This seems to bother a lot of people. They think because their idea is similar to someone else's idea that they actually *did* something with, that they are due some kind of compensation. Wrong. People don't get paid for having ideas. They get paid for what they *do* with those ideas. Don't make the rookie mistake of crying foul just because someone else publishes a story that is similar to an idea you once had.

Second, there's the script. The script is a typed collection of character dialogue, story and action notes, direction, and so on. A script *is* protected by copyright. Music (written on sheets) are also protected by copyright.

Lastly there's the movie itself. The movie is the edited video (including special effects, if any) and sound (dialogue, sound effects, music, etc.) all collected into a finished product. The movie is also protected by copyright.

How is a copyright different from a patent or a trademark?

Copyright protects original works of authorship, while a patent protects inventions or discoveries. Ideas and discoveries are not protected by the copyright law, although the way in which they are expressed may be. A trademark protects words, phrases, symbols, or designs identifying the source of the goods or services of one party and distinguishing them from those of others (source: copyright.gov).

Let's look at a bottle of Nutty Cola. The original recipe or "**formula**" for the Nutty Cola drink can be **patented** as an invention.

The **written expression** of the formula (but not the formula itself) would be protected by **copyright**.

The "Nutty Cola" **name and logo** would be considered a **trademark** (if used on packaging, advertising, etc.).

All three are "intellectual properties." The World Intellectual Property Organization defines intellectual property (IP) as "creations of the mind, such as inventions; literary and artistic works; designs; and symbols, names and images used in commerce."

When is my work protected?

Your work is under copyright protection the moment it is created and fixed in a tangible form that it is perceptible either directly or with the aid of a machine or device (source: copyright.gov).

If you're writing a novel, the moment your manuscript is finished, it's protected by copyright. You can even put a copyright notice on it, if you'd like. That's a notice that reads "copyright [year] by [name of owner]." Alternately you can put the "c in a circle" symbol (which means "copyright") along with the year and name of the owner, like this: "© 2017 Ima Writer."

Remember, "copyright" is a noun, not a verb. There is no act of "copyrighting" a work other than creating the work itself.

Having ownership of the copyright of a work allows you to proclaim ownership of the work. It does not, however, allow you to file a lawsuit against another party for infringing on your copyright, getting a court order to stop someone else from making and distributing copies of your work, or collect "damages" (monetary compensation for lost profits, etc., resulting from their illegal use of your work). For that you must register your copyright with the U.S. Copyright Office.

Do I have to register with the Copyright Office to be protected?

No. Registration of your copyright is voluntary. That's it. I'm not sure what else to say about it that isn't already mentioned somewhere else.

Why register if copyright protection is automatic?

Registration is recommended for several reasons. Registering your work allows you to have the facts of your copyright on the public record and provides you with a certificate of registration.

Registered works may be eligible for statutory damages and attorney's fees in a successful lawsuit.

Lastly, if you register your copyright within five (5) years of publication, it's considered *prima facie* evidence in court. A what, you say? "Prima facie" means there's rebuttable presumption that you are the copyright holder.

What is a "poor man's copyright?"

You've probably heard of mailing yourself a copy of your manuscript as some sort of "poor man's copyright." The idea is that the postmark can be used to "prove" when the work was created and that it is yours.

U.S. copyright law doesn't say anything about this tactic, which means it's nothing but a false rumor (albeit a widely circulated one). At best, the postmark on an unopened package establishes the absolute latest date the work could have been created. At worst it demonstrates that the person is naïve when it comes to copyright law.

Is my copyright good in other countries?

The United States has copyright relations with most countries throughout the world and, as a result of these agreements, they honor each other's citizens' copyrights. The U.S. doesn't have such copyright relationships with every country, however. For a listing of countries and the nature of their copyright relations with the United States, see Circular 38a, *International Copyright Relations of the United States*, which you can find at http://copyright.gov.

What is a Trademark?

A trademark is a brand name. A trademark or service mark includes any word, name, symbol, device, or any combination, used or intended to be used to identify and distinguish the goods/services of one seller or provider from those of others, and to indicate the source of the goods/services.

For information about trademarks, including some excellent informational videos about trademarks and patents, visit the United States Patent and Trademark Office web site at https://www.uspto.gov/trademark.

NOTES

"People say jargon is a bad thing, but it's really a shortcut vocabulary professionals use to understand one another."

—Erin McKean

Appendix 1: Glossary

A

AAP: Association of American Publishers, a trade association for US publishers.

ABA: American Booksellers Association.

Acknowledgments: The section of a book for the author to recognize key people who may have influenced the book or who are important to the author.

Acquiring Editor: Person in a publishing company who identifies and negotiates to acquire new titles for publication. The Acquiring Editor typically passes the manuscript to the development editor (unless they are the same person).

Advance: A payment made by a publisher to an author as an advance against future royalties. The advance is typically paid to an author in exchange for the rights to sell and publish their book. It's often paid in two parts: half upon signing the publishing contract and the rest upon delivery (or publisher's formal acceptance) of the manuscript. Royalties accrued from book sales must surpass the size of the advance for any additional royalties to be paid.

Advance copies: The first printed copies of a book intended to fill advance orders and special requests.

Afterword: Closing remarks by the author (or someone else), perhaps about the topic of the book or the process of writing it.

Agent: See Literary Agent.

AI: (sometimes AIS) Advance Information (Sheet), a document produced by publishers for new titles, such as a blurb, the author's biography and overview of their previous works, as well as the book's specifications, publication date, and price.

ALA: American Library Association.

Answer codes: Replies given by publishers' distribution centers on invoices to orders for books. These can include: out of print, not yet published, temporarily unavailable, and so on.

Appendix: Supplementary material appearing at the end of the book, not part of the main text, such as tables, statistical information, references, or other information.

ASIN: A version of an ISBN, used by a major online bookseller. An ASIN is assigned for free when publishing eBooks through the Kindle Direct Publishing platform.

Auction: A process where a title is submitted (typically by an agent) to multiple publishers in order to get the best offer.

Author biography: Personal information and accomplishments of the author.

B

Back matter: All printed material that appears in the back of the book after the body copy, including an afterword, appendix, bibliography, colophon, a glossary, and an index.

Backlist: An author or publisher's older and sometimes out-of-print titles.

Barcode: A machine readable image of lines encoding a book's ISBN, normally printed on the back cover of a book.

Back orders: Orders taken when a title is unavailable to be fulfilled when the book is back in stock.

Berne Conventions: An international agreement made in 1886 for the respect of copyright between participating nations.

Bibliography: A list of published books or articles cited as resources by the author.

Binding: The back cover, spine and front cover of a book; what holds a book together. Types of binding include: case binding, comb binding, perfect binding, saddle stitching, spiral binding, and velo binding.

Bleed: The portion of an illustration or image which extends beyond the trimmed page.

Blocking: the use of metallic foils, generally on covers and jackets, for visual impact.

Bluelines: (also known as "Blues.") A blueprint mock-up of all of the pages of the book, generated by the printer and printed from the final plates. Bluelines allow a final opportunity to find any errors and make minor corrections before the book goes to press. Any changes that are needed at this stage will require new films made, which can be expensive.

Blurb: A brief description of a book, used for marketing, which appears on the back of a paperback or on the inside front flap of a hardback. Sometimes referred to as "sell text," as it helps "sell" the book to potential buyers who read it.

Board books: Small, often square-shaped books with a small number of thick pages, intended for infants and toddlers.

Body copy: The majority of the text of the book. Body copy appears between the front and back matter.

Boilerplate: A publisher's standard contract, used as a starting point for negotiating final terms.

Book block: The sewn or perfect bound pages of a hardback book before they are bound to the case binding.

Book fair: An exhibition and convention for publishers, authors, or booksellers. There are many fairs that occur annually around the world.

Book manufacturing: The whole process of typesetting a book, printing it, binding it, and then packing it for shipping.

Book proof: A specially produced, advance copy of the uncorrected iteration of a book, intended for a limited audience, such as reviewers and buyers. (See also *review copy*).

Book proposal: Description of a proposed book that an author sends to a publisher, often including sample chapters and an outline.

Book signing: A publicized event, often held at bookstores or book fairs, featuring an author reading from (and perhaps discussing) the author's book and autographing the book for customers.

Book trailer: A video advertisement for a book, much like a movie trailer.

Jacket: The paper cover wrapped around a hardback book, typically laminated for durability in handling.

Bowker: (R. R. Bowker) The leading US bibliographical publishing company.

C

Camera ready copy: In traditional printing, this is the text of a title supplied to a printer, ready for reproduction and printing. In modern printing, it may refer to a digital file that is of the proper specifications and ready to be sent directly to a printer.

Case bound: A hardback/hardcover book.

Chapter books: A category of books aimed at children ages 9-12. Chapter books may include one line drawing per chapter but, unlike picture books, they use mostly text to tell a story.

Colophon: While it originally referred to the bibliographic information printed at the end of a book, the term is now used almost exclusively for the device or logo of the publisher.

Commissioning Editor: See Acquiring Editor.

Concept book: A picture book for preschool children that attempts to teach a basic concept, typically using illustrations and only a few words per page.

Consignment: Books sold on consignment are paid for as they are resold rather than invoiced.

Contract: A legal document detailing an author agreement to sell to a publisher some or all rights to a creative work. Contracts can be very lengthy and complex. It's always best to have a contract reviewed by an attorney before signing it. Also known as a publishing agreement.

Conversion: See *formatting*.

Copy Editor: An editor who works on the accuracy, style, consistency of formatting, and punctuation in a manuscript, ensuring accuracy and completeness, and preparing it for typesetting.

Copyright page: A page toward the front of the book containing the copyright notice. Typically, this page also includes cataloging data for libraries.

Copyright: The exclusive right to make copies, license, and otherwise exploit a work. Ideas cannot be protected by copyright; only the expression of those ideas.

Cover spread: The entire cover of a physical book, from the front, including the spine, to the back.

CRC: See Camera ready copy.

Critique: An evaluation of a manuscript, including structure, character and plot development.

D

Dedication: Part of the front matter containing the author's dedication of the book, typically to a person or number of people.

Development Editor: The editor who does the substantive editing of a book, with particular attention paid to overall style, pacing, plot, and structure. The development editor works with the author on revisions.

Dewey decimal system: the main system of library book classification.

Discount: the percentage reduction from the publisher's suggested retail price (SRP) at which a book is sold to a bookseller. Discounts as large as 50% are not uncommon.

Distribution: Making your book available to wholesalers, retailers, and readers.

Distributor: A company that stores, catalogs, sells and ships (distributes) books to retailers, libraries or wholesalers, on behalf of a publisher. Distributors keep a portion of sales and pass the rest to the publisher.

DPI: Dots per inch; the resolution of an image or text. Contemporary computer screens generally display at a resolution of 96 dpi, whereas 300 dpi is necessary for good print quality.

Draft: A book manuscript at a particular stage. The first draft is followed by rough drafts, which are unpolished versions. The final draft is sent to prepress.

Dust jacket: A detachable outer cover that protects the book, printed with the cover design. Usually for hardback/hardcover books.

E

.ePub: A file format used by many online book retailers.

EAN barcode: This barcode is the ISBN number transferred into machine-readable form.

eBook: An electronic version of a book, usually read on dedicated eReading devices such as Kindles or on devices such as smartphones, tablets, or PCs.

Edition: A specific version of a book.

Em: A typological measurement, so called because it represents the width of the widest character in the alphabet (i.e., the "M"). In general use, it is a synonym for pica em.

En: One half an em.

Endorsement: A written statement promoting an author or their book. Usually placed on the cover or in the front matter of the book, and used in marketing.

Endpaper: the pages of heavy cartridge paper at the front and back of a hardback book which join the book block to the hardback binding.

EPOS: Electronic Point Of Sale, the bookstore computer system used for sales data and stock control.

eRetailer: A retailer that sells print books or eBooks via the internet.

Errata: The correction of errors in a book. Once inserted as a slip of paper into the finished book, errata is today often listed as a page on a website.

Exclusivity: Part of a publishing contract binding the author to a single publisher. In the self-publishing industry, it means being exclusive to one particular store or retailer.

F

Fantasy: A genre of fiction. Fantasy stories bend or transcend the rules of the known world, and may include things like time travel, talking animals, and super-human creatures.

Fiction: Writing that comes from the imagination, or writing that does not adhere to the facts related to true events.

First edition: The first printing of a book.

Folio: The page number printed at the top or bottom of each printed page.

Footnote: An explanatory note inserted at the foot of the page, typically referring to a point within the text.

Fore-edge: the right-hand edge of a book when opened, opposite the spine.

Foreword: An introduction to a book, usually written by someone other than the author of the book.

Format: The shape of a book defined by its height and depth.

Formatting: The process of turning a manuscript file (like a Word document) into a format that can be published.

Frankfurt Book Fair: Arguably the most important international book fair of the year, especially for the buying and selling of rights. It is held in Frankfurt at the beginning of October.

Front list: Traditional, books released in the current season, in their first year of publication.

Front matter: The material preceding the beginning chapters of the book including the title page, copyright page, dedication, table of contents, foreword, preface, acknowledgment, and introduction.

Frontispiece: An illustration appearing before the first pages of a book, typically facing the title page.

G

galley: The interior text of a book, after all, editing and formatting're been done. It was once a term for a proof of lines of type prior to page make-up. *Origin:* The galley was the tray in which lines of metal type were assembled back when printing presses utilized hand or mechanical composition.

Genre: A category of books, denoted by content (e.g., fantasy, romance, or horror).

Ghostwriter: A person who writes books, articles and stories that are credited to another person. Celebrities often use ghostwriters for autobiographies and magazine articles.

Grayscale: An image solely composed of shades of black and gray.

H

Half-tone: Illustrations reproduced using black dots for printing.

Hardback/hardcover: A case bound book. Usually sewn and glued, hardcover books are then bound with cardboard covers reinforced with a stiff cloth, then wrapped with a paper dust jacket.

Headline: Also known as a running head, the line which appears at the top of each printed page, typically including the book title on the left side and chapter title on the right side.

Historical Fiction: Books in which the characters are fictional, but the setting and other details are rooted in actual history.

Imposition: the positioning of pages when printed, which produces the correct sequence of pages when folded.

Imprint: the name of the publisher under which a title is issued; the term often represents a publishing brand or division, rather than a publishing company. A publisher may have many imprints.

Independent bookstores: Retail stores, not owned by large companies that sell books to the general public.

InDesign: A graphic design and book layout software package from Adobe, popular with book designers who use PCs.

Index: An alphabetical listing of topics and keywords in a book (especially names, places, and events) and the pages on which they appear.

Ingram Book Group: a leading wholesaler of books, audiobooks, and periodicals to booksellers, librarians, and specialty retailers.

Institutional sales: Book sales primarily to schools and libraries, especially by children's book publishers.

In-Store or On-Sale Date: The date that a product arrives in the stores and is stocked on the shelves for customers to buy.

Interior graphics / images: All of the pictures, diagrams, figures and other images that appear within the interior.

Interior: All the content within the book; everything except the cover.

International Standard Book Number (ISBN): A unique 13-digit number (can be 10 or 13 digits if issued prior to 2007) that identifies a specific edition of a book or eBook. The system provides a standard way for publishers to number their products without duplication by other publishers.

International Standard Serial Number (ISSN): A worldwide numbering system for periodicals and other serially-produced products.

IPA: International Publishers Association; an organization representing the publishing industry around the world.

J

Jacket: The paper cover wrapped around a hardback.

Keyword: An important word or phrase that can be assigned to a book, used by search engines and readers looking for genres, authors, etc.

Kill fee: A payment made to an author or illustrator when a publisher cancels a project.

Kindle Direct Publishing: A platform provided by Amazon to authors. KDP allows authors to make books available on Kindle and other retail outlets.

Kindle: An eReader platform produced by *Amazon*.

Lamination: the coating of film applied to book jackets to provide a high gloss and added durability. A matte version is also available.

Landscape: a format which is wider than it is tall.

Large print: editions of existing titles redesigned for reading by those with impaired vision, often produced for the library market.

Layout: The overall design of a book's pages, including the arrangement of text, font/typeface, page numbers, images and graphics, and so on.

Leaf: a page of the book comprising both recto and verso.

Library of Congress: the USA's national book collection, based in Washington, DC.

licence: a subsidiary right, usually granted for a fixed term or for a particular usage.

Limited Edition: A book printed in limited numbers, regardless of demand, usually for special editions.

Line Editor: An editor who performs an edit that is heavier than the usual copyedit, focusing on voice, tone, or phrasing. A line editor may also focus on grammar, punctuation and writing style.

List: Books designated for publication in a particular sales season.

List price: The cover price of a book, also called the "retail" price. (See also *suggested retail price*.

Literary agent: See *agent*.

Literary Market Place: A publication by Bowker listing US publishers and other book trade information. An international edition is also published.

M

.Mobi: A proprietary eBook file format, for use on Kindle devices and apps.

Machine readable code: see *barcode*.

Manuscript: An author's complete version of a book before it's typeset and printed. MS and MSS are shorthand designations for "manuscript" or "manuscripts."

Margin: the white space surrounding a page of type.

Market: 1. the potential readership for a title. 2. The territories of the world in which a book title may be contractually distributed and sold.

Marketing: The process of promoting and advertising a book to maximize sales.

Mass market paperback: A smaller (4 and 3/16" x 6 and 3/4") paperback book usually printed on low-grade paper and released in high quantity at a lower price than a trade paperback. In addition to bookstores, these "rack sized" books are often sold in drugstores, airports, and supermarkets.

Match print: a brand name for a common form of digital color proof.

Mechanical: a paper made from mechanically treated wood pulp, which has a limited life and tends to discolor with time. It was originally used only for paperbacks and other titles of limited value.

Media Kit / Press Kit: A folder containing promotional materials for announcing information about a forthcoming book to the news media and other targeted outlets.

Merchandising: the management of stock in supermarkets and other non-specialist sales outlets to ensure displaying the fastest selling titles.

Middle Reader: Books geared for readers aged 9-11.

Midlist: Books that have a chance of significant success but not assumed to be likely bestsellers.

N

National Book Network: The largest independent distributor in North America. NBN provides sales, marketing, order fulfillment, and credit and collection services to independent publishers of commercial fiction and nonfiction books.

New edition: a reprint of an existing title with substantial changes to the text or a new printing of a previously out-of-print title.

Nonfiction: Writing in which the author retells actual events.

Nook: A brand of eReader developed by *Barnes & Noble*.

Novelty book: Books with special built-in features such as pop-ups, foldout pages, hidden sound chips, and so on.

NYP: common abbreviation for Not Yet Published; see answer codes.

O

Offset printing: Traditional printing technology where ink is transferred from a roller to a printing surface, and then to a page of a book. Typically used for large print runs.

OP: The universal abbreviation for Out of Print (see *answer codes*). When a publisher has no copies of a book left and no intent to reprint it.

Option clause: A clause in a contract giving a publisher the right to consider acquiring the author's next book before other publishers are given the opportunity.

Out of Stock Indefinitely (OSI): Status of a book when the publisher has no copies of a specific title on hand, but may desire to reprint it in the future.

Overrun: The excess quantity of books when a print run is larger than the one ordered. There's a "standard" 10% overrun in traditional printing orders, printed to offset possible defective or damaged copies ("spoilage").

P

Pantone: brand name of an ink-matching system widely used by designers for color specification.

Portable Document Format (PDF): A popular and widely-used file format produced by *Adobe Systems*. All formatting and style is preserved in the file.

Perfect binding: A type of binding where the pages are glued at the spine to a cardstock paper cover (thus the more common name "paperback").

Picture Book: Picture books are typically 24 to 32 pages long and primarily aimed at children from preschool to age 8. They display illustrations on every page, telling the story through images accompanied by at most a few lines of text.

Plates: These are illustrations printed separately from the main text of a book and inserted in the appropriate place by the binder.

point of sale (POS): merchandising display material provided by publishers to bookstores to promote particular titles.

Point: A measurement for type; twelve points equal one pica em. Most books are set in 10- or 11-point type.

Portrait: A page format that's taller than it is wide.

PP&B: Paper, Printing, and Binding.

Preface: An introductory section of a book, usually written by the author.

Prelims: The preliminary pages of a book, prior to the start of the main text. The prelims are often numbered in roman numerals.

Prepress: The steps required to prepare a book for the printer. High-end book design software includes prepress packaging of necessary files for professional printers.

Press release: A formal written announcement designed to attract media attention to a specific event or product launch.

Print run: The number of copies of a product (e.g., book) printed in a single order.

Printer's errors: Mistakes made by the printer during manufacturing (e.g., incorrectly trimmed pages, smudges, smears, or unintended ink-blots on pages).

Print-on-Demand (POD): A publishing process in which books are printed in small quantities and only to fill placed orders, eliminating the need for (and cost of) storing inventory.

Process colors: Four colors used in the analog printing process to represent the full spectrum. They are Cyan (blue), Magenta (red), Yellow, and black, abbreviated as CMYK.

Proof: A copy of a book or cover produced so it can be checked by the publisher or author for errors. (See also *book proof*.)

Proofreader: An editor employed to examine proof copies to check for accuracy and proper formatting.

Public domain: Works not legally protected as intellectual property, including those whose protection has expired, are said to be in the "public domain." Anyone may reproduce, sell or otherwise use a public domain work without requiring permission to do so.

Publication date: The official date when the publisher announces that a book will be available.

Publishers Group West: the largest exclusive distributor of independent publishers in North America. One of the top ten vendors of books in the country, Publishers Group West represents over 150 independent publishers.

Publishers Weekly: the journal of the US book trade, published by Bowker.

Q

QuarkXPress: a graphic design and book layout software package, popular with book designers who use Macs.

Query letter: A letter from an author or agent to an editor briefly describing a manuscript and asking if the editor is interested in evaluating the manuscript.

R

Reading fee: A fee charged by some agents to evaluate a prospective client's manuscript, considered unethical in some circles.

Suggested retail price (SRP): The price the publisher recommends a book be sold, to which the bookseller's wholesale discount is applied, and upon which royalties to the author are traditionally calculated.

Recto: the right-hand page of an opening in a book.

Register: the accurate printing of each of the four process colors (CMYK) on top of the others to produce a printed color image.

Remainder copies: Copies of a book that are deeply discounted for fast turnover, often due to low sales or excess stock. Often sold through bargain bookshops etc.

Reprint: a second or subsequent printing of a title.

Return: A book that fails to sell or has become damaged, and is returned to the publisher for full credit.

Review copies: Books that are provided to reviewers, usually in advance of the book's official release.

Review: A published opinion of a work. It may be from a professional book reviewer or an amateur (a reader).

Revisions: Changes to an original work; may be simple or extensive.

Subsidiary rights: The rights to distribute a book through book clubs, in foreign translated editions, through excerpts in newspapers and magazines, as a movie adaptation, and so on.

Royalties: A percentage of the book's sale price that's paid to the author or illustrator.

S

Standard Account Number (SAN): A number assigned to libraries, schools, and other organizations that buy, sell, or lend books.

Screen: the process of breaking down a photographic image into dots for printing.

Self-publishing: A form of publishing used by authors, employing electronic publishing platforms and POD printers to bypass the traditional publishing model, reaching consumers and markets directly.

Sell text: See *blurb*.

Sheet-fed: printing term for a machine printing on individual sheets of paper (instead of a large industrial-sized roll).

Signature: Printers' term for a large sheet of paper that, when printed, folded and trimmed, makes up a number of pages. Typically, 16 pages make up a signature (the number will always be a multiple of 4). Not used much since the advent of digital printing.

Slipcase: A cardboard box, open at one end, into which one or more books are inserted.

Slush pile: Term for the unsolicited manuscripts sent to publishers and agents, often not read.

Special sales: Non-traditional sales to outlets that don't specialize in books (such as gift shops, pet shops, etc.).

Spine: The bound edge of a book that faces out when shelved, where the title, author's and publisher's name normally appear.

Spiral-bound: A type of binding where wire or plastic is spiraled through holes punched along the binding side of a book.

Spoilage: Planned paper waste; traditionally printers estimate 10% of a print run will be spoilage.

Spot varnish: The application of varnish to limited parts of a cover or jacket (e.g., just to the title) for visual impact.

Submissions: Manuscripts sent by an author or agent to a publisher for consideration.

T

Table of Contents: A section in the front matter of a book, listing the topics covered in the book as arranged by chapter and section, and including the page numbers.

Target audience: A specific demographic of readers or segment of a market likely to be interested in a particular book.

Territory: Different geographical regions for which authors and publishers can license and own different rights.

Title page: The odd-numbered, right-hand page that lists the book's title, subtitle, and author's name.

Title verso: the reverse of the title-page, on which the publisher's name and address, ISBN and other bibliographical details are typically printed.

Trade bookseller: A bookseller which distributes books to the general public.

Trade discount: See *wholesale discount.*

Trade paperback: Books that are larger than mass market paperback books and bound with a heavy paper cover. They're often the same size and have the same cover design as the hardcover edition.

Trademark: A brand name; includes any word, name, symbol, device, or combination, used to identify the source goods/services.

Translation rights: the right acquired to translate and publish a work into another language.

Trim size: The outer dimensions of a finished print book.

Typeface: The design of the individual characters making up the text of a book.

Typesetting: The process of arranging the interior text of a book to make it ready to be printed.

U

Underrun: A finished order containing fewer books than ordered. This can result from excessive spoilage during printing or from printer's errors.

Unit cost: The base cost of printing and binding a book.

UV varnish: A varnish cured by ultraviolet light, normally applied to book covers and jackets as part of the printing process.

V

Verso: the reverse of a page in a book.

W

Web offset: A printing process, which prints onto a reel or web of paper, and produces folded sections of the press.

Wholesale discount: The reduced price at which retailers or distributors buy books from a publisher.

Wholesaler: A company that buys books from publishers at high discounts, then sells them to bookstores and libraries.

Y

YA Books: Books are most often targeted at readers ages 12-18.

About Mark

Mark Arsenault is a John Maxwell Certified Coach, Trainer, and Speaker. He is also the founder of Success Revolution, a company dedicated to bringing positive mindset and motivational training to individuals and organizations. He is also the founding Director of GAATES, Inc., a 501(c)(3) nonprofit dedicated to reducing recidivism and helping ex-offenders through personal development, career readiness, and success strategies.

Mark is a best-selling and award-winning author of a number of books, including *Beat the Curve*, with Brian Tracy, and *Semicolon; Memoir of a Colon Cancer Survivor*. He is an avid reader and an amateur historian, having studied Asian cultures with a focus on feudal Japan. Mark has studied, researched, written and spoken for more than fifteen years in the fields of history, business, corrections, and psychology.

He's been quoted in *SUCCESS Magazine*, *USA Today*, *The Wall Street Journal*, *The Washington Post* and *The New York Times*. He also appeared in a national anti-smoking public service announcement in 2015.

Prior to founding his company, Success Revolution, Mark had a successful career in law enforcement and corrections, where he co-created and co-facilitated a successful in-custody gang diversion and mindset program for state and county inmates. He's also run a successful publishing business and is a decorated U.S. Air Force veteran of Desert Shield and Desert Storm.

Mark is happily married and has two children. He is active in the community and donated time as a volunteer speaker with several community programs as a way to "pay forward" what he's gained from his study of personal development.

Follow Mark's blog at **http://MarkTruth.com**

98

Best-selling author Mark T. Arsenault, presents Think Up!, a collection of short articles and blog posts designed to help readers look beyond their circumstances, achieve a positive mindset and reach their goals.

The articles in Think Up! first appeared in Mark's successful blog, Join Me For Success, which had thousands of visitors every month. The articles have been collected and appear in print for the first time in Think Up!

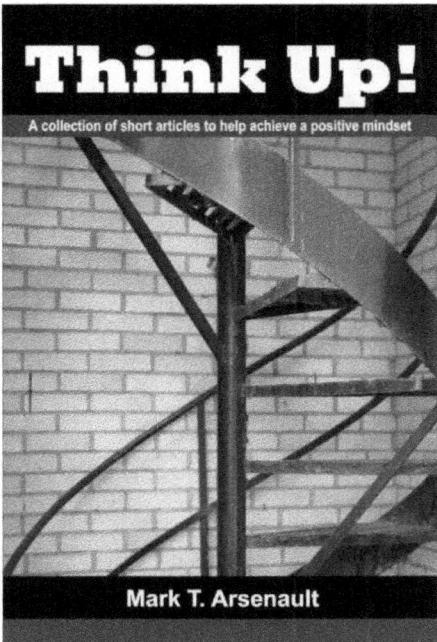

Available now at Amazon.com and other booksellers!

Available in print and eBook.

Published by
Gold Rush Publishing
www.GoldRushPub.com

www.ingramcontent.com/pod-product-compliance
Lightning Source LLC
Chambersburg PA
CBHW071618040426
42452CB00009B/1388